EXTRAORDINARY ANIMALS!

Written by
William O'Byrne

HORWITZ
MARTIN
EDUCATION

Contents

Special Note:
The animals featured in this book provide factual support for the animals in the two related Tristars fiction books:
- ★ *Grandad's Wild Stories*
- ★ *Zoo Trip!*

Each Animal Is Unique!

M ost of us have watched wildlife programs on TV or we have visited a wildlife park, a zoo or a national park. So it's possible we may have seen all of the following animals:

* Crocodiles
* Snakes
* Lions
* Wolves

* Polar bears
* Grizzly bears
* Giraffes
* Kangaroos

Every animal is unique, and even the most ordinary animal has special features, if you look closely enough. In this book, we'll look at some well-known animals and discover some extraordinary features in each of them.

Chapter 1

Reptiles

Reptiles, such as snakes, lizards, crocodiles, turtles, and the tuatara, all share certain characteristics. All reptiles are vertebrates, which means they have a backbone. Their young grow from eggs, which are laid on land, even if the adults usually live in water. All reptiles have a skin covered in tough scales. Unlike birds and mammals, reptiles don't use food to keep their body temperature at a comfortable level. Instead, they use heat from the sun to keep themselves warm.

There are about 600 different species of reptiles alive today. But millions of years ago, reptiles were the most advanced kind of animal on earth.

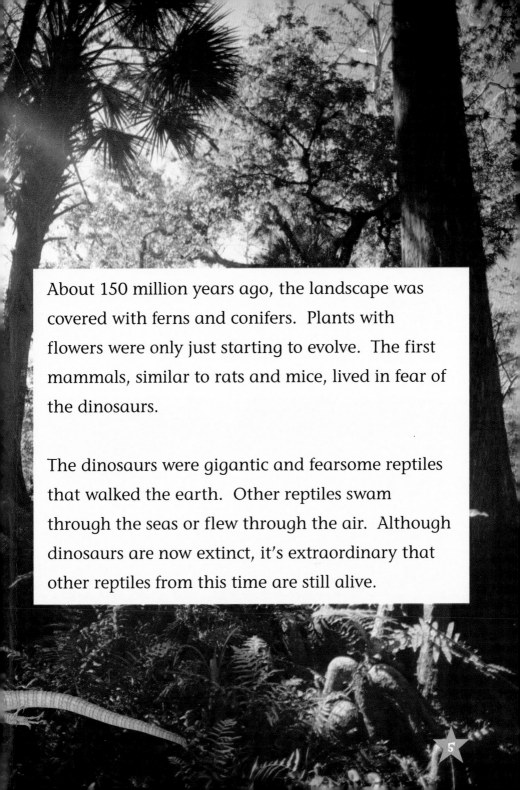

About 150 million years ago, the landscape was covered with ferns and conifers. Plants with flowers were only just starting to evolve. The first mammals, similar to rats and mice, lived in fear of the dinosaurs.

The dinosaurs were gigantic and fearsome reptiles that walked the earth. Other reptiles swam through the seas or flew through the air. Although dinosaurs are now extinct, it's extraordinary that other reptiles from this time are still alive.

Ancient Alligators and Crafty Crocodiles

Alligators and crocodiles have been around even longer than dinosaurs, first appearing on earth almost 250 million years ago. Silently, they waited for their prey to walk or swim past. Then, with lightning speed, they would surge forward and snap their giant jaws around their prey. These ancient reptilian predators were so well adapted to their shallow, salty environment that, today, their descendants still wait silently, hidden beneath the murky waters of many rivers and estuaries.

An alligator.

What's The Difference?

What's the difference between an alligator and a crocodile?

It's easy to tell — as long as they have their mouths shut! An alligator has no bottom teeth showing when it shuts its mouth. But the fourth tooth of a crocodile's lower jaw sticks out on either side of its closed mouth!

A crocodile.

The prize for the largest living reptile goes to the saltwater crocodile, found in rivers and estuaries from southern India to Australia. Most saltwater crocodiles grow to a length of five metres, but some that have been measured are as long as eight metres!

Alligators and crocodiles lay their eggs in nests they have dug out from soil or sand near the water. Unlike many other reptiles, they tend to stay near their nests, to keep predators away. Amazingly, the temperature of the air and soil around the nest determines whether the eggs hatch into male or female babies!

After baby crocodiles hatch, they are cared for by their mother. No other reptiles look after their young. Often, the young are gently protected from predators inside their mother's mouth.

Alligator and Crocodile Facts

- Older than dinosaurs. That's extraordinary!
- The largest living reptiles.

  That's extraordinary!
- Can be born male or female, depending on the outside temperature.

  That's extraordinary!
- Dangerous carnivores, yet caring parents.

  That's extraordinary!

Slithering Snakes

Like crocodiles, snakes are also reptiles. They have all the features of other reptiles, except for legs! Snakes evolved much later than crocodiles, first appearing on earth about 140 million years ago.

One of the oldest snake fossils we have found is of an enormous sea snake. It was 24 metres long — four times as long as the longest snake living today, the python.

In a human, 24 separate bones, called vertebrae, make up our backbone. Small snakes have about 180, while the longest snakes can have up to 400 vertebrae! This means they can be very flexible. Snakes move on land by bending themselves into an 'S' shape and pushing their bodies along against a surface.

The skeleton of a snake also has another extraordinary feature. Snakes can unhook their jaws so that their mouths can stretch over animals or eggs twice as wide as the snake itself!

A green Brazilian snake.

Some snakes, such as cobras and rattlesnakes, kill their prey by injecting it with poison from two fangs at the front of their mouths. Others, like pythons, kill their prey by wrapping themselves around the animal and squeezing it until it cannot breathe.

Snakes use an amazing combination of senses to find their prey. Most snakes have very poor eyesight and no external ears. Instead, they have a simple ear inside their bodies, which is not as effective as the ears of most other animals. So, without being able to see or hear their meals approaching, how do snakes manage to survive?

A snake can detect animals by 'tasting' the air around itself with its very sensitive forked tongue. Just as we can smell things, a snake can taste something approaching from a distance. Its tongue can detect molecules given off by animals, in the same way our noses detect molecules in the air.

A cobra, ready to strike.

Some snakes can even sense the heat given off by a warm-blooded animal like a mammal or a bird. They have tiny holes in their lips that can sense heat. Together with the ability to 'taste' an animal in the distance, this is very useful for snakes that like to hunt at night!

A rattlesnake.

A snake shedding its skin.

The scales on reptiles are tough and leathery, so it is not easy for them to stretch or grow. This means that, as reptiles grow larger, they need to replace their skins. Snakes grow a new skin underneath their old one, and then wriggle out of it when the old skin feels too tight! Young snakes can slither out of their old skins as many as seven times in their first year! Each skin change usually takes about half an hour. That's an extraordinary amount of changing skins, even for a reptile!

Snake Facts

- Able to move without legs. That's extraordinary!
- Able to swallow food twice their size. That's extraordinary!
- Able to 'taste' the air, and detect heat from other animals. That's extraordinary!
- Able to wriggle out of their skins in half an hour. That's extraordinary!

Chapter 2

Wild Cats and Dogs

C ats, dogs, tigers and wolves all belong to a group of animals called 'Carnivora'. This means they are carnivorous, or mostly meat-eating. These animals, as well as humans, belong to a bigger group called mammals. All mammals are warm-blooded, they have fur, and as babies they drink milk from their mothers. All mammals, except for the platypus and echidna, are born alive, not from eggs.

Mammals first appeared about 200 million years ago, but it wasn't until the dinosaurs died out that their populations increased. When dinosaurs became extinct, many mammals simply took their place.

About 45 million years ago, a fearsome group of carnivores appeared. With their large teeth, extreme speed and sharp claws, they were extraordinary hunting machines. They were the first cats.

Lazy Lions

One of the best known cat carnivores today is the lion. But it may surprise you to know that a powerful lion can sleep for up to 18 hours a day — just like a pet cat does! Male lions rest even more than female lions. The females usually do all the hunting, while the males wait for their food!

Unlike most other cats, lions prefer to live in groups, or 'prides'. A pride can consist of up to 30 males, females and cubs. Prides usually stay in the same area. Each pride may live in an area of about 100 square kilometres.

It can be dangerous being a young cub in a pride. Up to one-third of all lion cubs are killed and eaten by older male lions!

Lion Facts

★ **Sleep for up to 18 hours a day.**
That's extraordinary!

★ **Are the only cats that live in groups.**
That's extraordinary!

★ **Males sometimes eat their cubs.**
That's extraordinary!

Wandering Wolves

The first dogs were probably very similar to wolves. Although we may think that dogs are tame animals, they still behave like wolves in many ways. Dogs were probably the first animals to be domesticated. People and dogs learned to live together from about 10,000 years ago.

Wolves are the largest of wild dogs, growing up to two metres from nose to tail and almost a metre tall. They can survive in very harsh climates, like those found in the forests close to the arctic. In fact, wolves were common during the Ice Age, 40,000 years ago. They shared the forests and plains with animals that are now extinct, such as the mammoth and the woolly rhinoceros.

Like all dogs, wolves prefer to live in packs, sharing out jobs like hunting and looking after their young. Domestic dogs also like to live in packs — but humans often make up the rest of their pack, instead of other dogs. A wolf pack may have up to twenty wolves, all living and sleeping together. They are led by the oldest or the strongest wolf. Domestic dog packs may be led by the oldest or strongest human — or, at least, the human who knows where the food is kept!

Each wolf pack has its own territory, where it roams to hunt other animals. Wolves howl at night to warn other wolves to keep away from their territory. Wolf territories can be larger than 1,000 square kilometres. In their territory, wolves work together to hunt and catch animals many times larger than themselves, such as deer, wild cattle, or caribou. The wolves force herds of deer, cattle or caribou to move around until one animal separates from the rest. Then they catch the lone animal.

When a pack of hunting wolves returns to their camp, the other wolves bark and howl in excitement. They know the hunter wolves are bringing food, or news of where they have hidden some food. A pet dog behaves in the same way when their human family returns home. The dog will become excited, and bark a greeting.

A wolf cub, howling.

Wolves are extraordinary because, unlike most wild animals, they will usually choose one partner for their whole lives. Together, these two wolves will have wolf cubs. The cubs, when they grow up, may choose to stay in the wolf pack or find another one. When the strongest or oldest wolf becomes too weak to lead the pack, one of the younger wolves will take over. If there is not enough food for a whole wolf pack, it may split up into smaller packs, with new leaders.

Wolf Facts

* **The ancestors of our pet dogs.** That's extraordinary!
* **Able to live and hunt together in packs, each with a different job.** That's extraordinary!
* **Only choose one partner for their whole lives. For wild animals,** that's extraordinary!

Chapter 3

Bears

Bears are also mammals, and they are also grouped in the carnivore family — even though many bears eat a lot of leaves, fruit and nuts in their diet. An unusual bear, the panda bear, eats only bamboo leaves, but it is still classed as a carnivore!

A panda bear.

When humans first started living in caves, they found they had some rather grumpy neighbours. Giant cave bears lived throughout Europe and North America. These were fearsome bears almost twice as big as the grizzly bears that live in North America today. They became extinct about 20,000 years ago.

A black bear.

Preying Polar Bears

In the arctic regions, far in the northern part of the world, the sun never rises during winter. It is dark all day long, and the icy lands are freezing cold. To avoid the extreme temperatures of the arctic winter, each polar bear builds a snow cave, called a den. During hibernation, their body temperature lowers, and the movement of their heart and lungs slows down.

For many female polar bears, cubs are growing inside them during hibernation. About a month after they begin to live in their winter dens, their cubs are born. For the next three months, female polar bears feed them milk from their body.

When spring arrives, the whole family dig themselves out of their den. The polar bear cubs are fat and healthy — but the mothers are thin and hungry. The first thing they must do is find something to eat after their long, four-month fast!

Polar bear cubs spend two to three years with their mother. She will teach them how to hunt, and she will protect them from preying polar bears. Male polar bears will sometimes attack and kill cubs.

Polar bears.

Although a polar bear looks white, it actually has black skin. Black attracts heat, and the skin helps to keep the polar bear warm. The white fur is really made up of transparent, hollow hairs. These hairs can transfer up to 95 percent of the sun's warmth straight to the skin. In an environment where the temperature can drop to minus 70 degrees Celsius, this is very useful!

Polar bears are great hitchhikers — but they don't wait for passing cars or trucks to pick them up! As the arctic summer warms up the frozen ice that covers the sea, large flat chunks of ice, called ice floes, break off. Ice floes can float for hundreds of kilometres in different directions. A polar bear will often climb on board a floating ice floe and travel great distances without walking or swimming anywhere. On the journey, it will eat seals and fish that it catches from the edge of its travelling home.

Polar Bear Facts

* Live in snow caves for the first three months of their lives. That's extraordinary!
* Are actually black, not white. That's extraordinary!
* Hitch rides on floating blocks of ice. That's extraordinary!

Great Grizzly Bears

Grizzly bears are the largest and most dangerous bears in North America. They are also known as brown bears or, in Alaska, as Kodiak bears. Although rare, they also live in Europe and Asia. They can grow almost three metres long, and weigh up to 750 kilograms.

Usually, grizzly bears will avoid humans, but they love human food, especially sweet food such as cake, biscuits, fruit and chocolate. Unfortunately, these are foods that many hikers and campers take with them into the forest. Experienced campers know to store their food somewhere safe, away from their tent. Grizzly bears can smell these foods from a great distance, and will do almost anything to taste them. That includes attacking humans who are in their way!

A grizzly bear.

Amazingly, bears and humans share a very interesting feature. They are the only animals that walk on the soles of their feet. Every other animal walks on its toes! But a hungry grizzly can easily outrun a human, with speeds of almost 40 kilometres an hour.

While bears and humans don't get on very well, sometimes bears will get along very well with other bears. Mother grizzly bears will sometimes team up with other mother grizzlies and form a sort of crèche, like a 'mother's group'.

The mother bears will take turns at minding each other's cubs, even feeding them milk from their bodies and teaching them how to hunt and survive. If one mother bear dies, the cubs may be adopted by the other mother bears until they are strong and old enough to look after themselves.

Grizzly Bear Facts

- Bears have a sweet tooth. That's extraordinary!
- Form 'mothers' groups' to look after, teach and feed their cubs. That's extraordinary!
- The only animal apart from humans to actually walk on the soles of their feet. That's extraordinary!

Chapter 4

Giraffes and Kangaroos

What's one of the main differences between horses and sheep, rhinos and hippos, or donkeys and deer? Horses, rhinos and donkeys all belong to a family of mammals that have an *odd* number of toes that are formed into hooves.

Sheep, hippos and deer all have an *even* number of toes. Other even-numbered hoofed animals include pigs, camels, llamas, goats and giraffes.

Giant Giraffes

The long neck of the giraffe enables an adult giraffe to reach as high as five and a half metres for the leaves that it eats as part of its diet.

Although the giraffe's neck may be two metres long, it has the same number of bones as a human's neck — only seven. And, although its long neck is extraordinary, the giraffe has another feature that helps it to graze off the leaves at the top of trees. It has a tongue that is almost 30 centimetres long! The tongue is able to twist around branches and twigs to pull them down towards its mouth.

Once the giraffe's tongue has pulled the branches into its mouth, the giraffe uses special grooved teeth to strip off the leaves. Then, the tough branches spring back up, minus the leaves. The giraffe's tongue and teeth are like a specialised leaf-stripping machine!

Giraffes live in Africa, alongside lions and other predators, so they must protect themselves against attack. One of the main ways they do this is by camouflage. The patterns on a giraffe's skin blend in well with the shadows cast by the leaves of the trees that they like to feed on. To a lion, a giraffe standing under a tree might appear invisible or camouflaged! Every giraffe has a different patterned skin.

A mother giraffe will also spend a lot of time licking and cleaning her baby giraffe. This helps to get rid of the giraffe scent that might attract predators like lions. If the camouflage and the cleaning doesn't work, an adult giraffe can use its back legs to kick a lion. Their huge 30 centimetre hooves can easily kill one!

A giraffe's legs are almost two metres long. When a baby giraffe is born, its legs are so wobbly, it takes about half an hour for it to work out how to stand up. But once giraffes become used to their long legs, they can run extremely fast. Running at a top speed of over 50 kilometres an hour, giraffes can run faster than many racehorses!

To keep blood flowing around such a tall body, the giraffe has a huge heart. The muscles that make up the heart are over seven centimetres thick, and they can move up to 110 litres of blood with each beat! To carry so much blood around, the giraffe's veins and arteries can be as wide as two and a half centimetres in diameter!

Bouncing Bush Kangaroos

Kangaroos belong to a very special group of mammals called marsupials. Marsupials are mostly found in Australia, except for possums, which can also be found in North and South America and New Zealand. Marsupials have a pouch where very young tiny babies are protected and fed. Instead of developing inside the mother's body, like most other mammals, marsupials spend most of their development time in their mother's pouch.

Like all marsupials, baby kangaroos (called joeys) are born much less developed than other mammals. They develop inside the mother for about five weeks, before they are born. The tiny deaf, blind and hairless joey, the same size and shape as a jellybaby, must crawl up its mother's stomach to find the pouch. There, it will live and grow for the next three to nine months.

A kangaroo can have up to three joeys of different ages growing inside her pouch at one time. The mother will feed each joey a different type of milk, depending on how old it is. The younger joeys drink a milk that is high in protein, to help them grow strong and healthy. The older joeys drink high-fat milk, which gives them plenty of energy to move around and strengthen their muscles.

Once the joeys become adults, they can grow almost two metres tall. The tail of a kangaroo can be up to three metres long, and is used for balance when the kangaroo is hopping around. While hopping may seem a slow way to move, large red kangaroos can hop at speeds of over 55 kilometres an hour. They can jump as far as nine metres in a single bound, and can jump over fences that are two or three metres high! That's quite a hop!

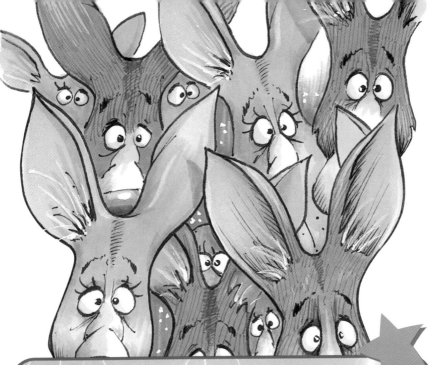

Kangaroo Facts

* Grow in safe pouches from the time they are born. **That's extraordinary!**

* Joeys have a choice of high-fat or high-protein milk from their mothers. **That's extraordinary!**

* Can hop in nine metre leaps, at speeds higher than the speed limit in most cities. **That's extraordinary!**

Ordinary or Extraordinary?

No matter how familiar we may be with wild animals, through pictures, TV, or visits to places where they live, they are never ordinary. Every animal has its own extraordinary features, developed to help them survive in the world we all share. That's what makes the world of nature on our planet so interesting — and worth taking care of. If an animal — any animal — becomes extinct, then we lose a creature that is truly extraordinary!

Glossary

ancestors
Family members who lived in the past.

arctic
The area around the North Pole.

caribou
A North American reindeer.

characteristics
Special shapes, features or behaviours.

conifers
Trees that have cones, e.g., pine trees.

descendants
Family members who live in the future, i.e., children, and their children.

detect
To find or sense.

diameter
The size (width) of a circle or tube.

estuaries
An estuary is the wide part of a river, where it joins the sea.

evolve
Change shape over time.

extinct
No longer any members of this species alive.

fossils
The ancient remains of animals or plants that have turned to stone over millions of years.

hibernation
The act of sleeping, or doing no activity, all winter.

molecules
Very small amounts of a chemical substance.

populations
Numbers of people or animals living in a certain place.

predators
Animals that kill and eat other animals.

prey
The animals that predators eat.

species
Types of plants or animals that belong to the same group, and are able to breed together.

transparent
See through.

Index